LIVING WITH BOOKS

For Pierre Paulin and Charlotte Perriand,
and Guillaume Sennelier, a keen reader without a library.

LIVING WITH BOOKS

Roland Beaufre
Dominique Dupuich

Thames & Hudson

Contents

Fashion designers
AND THEIR BOOKS

STYLISH & **GLAMOROUS**

Journalists
AND THEIR BOOKS

INTERNATIONAL & **UP-TO-DATE**

Artists
AND THEIR BOOKS

UNUSUAL & **INSPIRING**

Grand houses
AND THEIR BOOKS

IMPOSING & **AUTHORITATIVE**

Introduction

THE ART OF LIVING WITH BOOKS

All long-term love affairs require a little organization, and relationships between people and books are no different. It can't be denied that we love books, and what's more, we love them with an obsessive passion that can transcend our social and professional environment, one reason why it is so difficult to categorize the many ways that we we live with books. Book-collecting is an intimate, almost secret, passion, with bibliophiles part of a secret fraternity that is both real and intangible. Some people are almost walking libraries in themselves.

But any passion for the written word also has to be reconciled with the collector's lifestyle, as books can be compromising objects that one would not necessarily want to leave lying around. Between the art of order and the art of disorder lies a whole spectrum of nuances, comprising styles that can be ostentatious or even intimidating. At one end are the aristocrats of book collecting, connoisseurs in the grand style, with their perfectly aligned collections of antique books; at the other are the bohemians, fierce defenders of 'creative disorder', voracious readers and staunch opponents of handling books with kid gloves. A distinction can therefore be drawn between the purists (firm believers in the complete separation of books and the rest of the house, for whom the bookcase is sacrosanct) and the eclectics, for whom the bookcase is just another useful or decorative piece of furniture, in which the books may or may not remain. In any case, regardless of tradition or modernity, style or design, what really matters is the collector's relationship with his or her books.

This particular book provides a unique insight into the world of book lovers, taking us directly into the private homes of collectors, designers, interior designers, writers, fashion designers, journalists, artists and stately home owners. As well as describing the characteristics of the collectors in each of these eight categories, we will also look more closely at a specific example of each type of approach to book collecting.

White shelves, white walls, white computers: this home office, which belongs to Florence Müller, fashion historian and curator at the Institut Français de la Mode, is both modern and minimalist. The only ornaments are the gilt-edged mirror and miniature portrait gallery above the sofa.

Collectors
AND THEIR BOOKS
OBSESSIVE & DISCREET

Whether they are curators, ethnologists, publishers, gallery owners or historians, all book collectors have one thing in common: they are obsessed with rare books. Their goal is not to create an academic or research library, but to build up their own private collection. Collectors hunt and forage for whichever rare item they have set their sights on, determined not to return empty-handed; once they have their prey, it is for their eyes only, a purely selfish pleasure. Permanently dissatisfied, collectors buy, sell, resell and throw away, but never swap. Whether it is a minimalist monograph, an iconoclastic encyclopedia, a humble magazine or an old-fashioned novel, they seek the unusual, the incongruous and the unknown, steering clear of the well known and the obvious.

A small, intimate museum; a minutely controlled art gallery just for one. Both curator and visitor, the book collector has a lifestyle that has to constantly change in order to fit in with the ever-growing collection. Whether it is ultra-selective or obsessively exhaustive – which will depend on whether the collector is an introvert or an extrovert – the collection *is* the décor, not the other way around. Cupboards, cabinets, alcoves, recesses, bookcases and trunks are all of secondary importance. It does not matter if the collection is large or small, as far as the owner is concerned it is a private shrine, to be decorated with treasured objects, works of art, statues, talismans. A collection within a collection.

Book lover Emmanuel Pierrat's collection of African totems keeps watch over his books.

|1| |2|

|3|

|1/2/3| Every wall in Pierrat's home, from the hallway to the sitting room to the bedrooms, is covered with shelves made of exotic wood. Piles of books lie stacked up everywhere, like totems dedicated to learning, while in front of the large bookcase, two white wicker travelling chests, containing yet more books, make handy reading stools.

|1/2| In this completely white apartment in Paris, overlooking the Viaduc des Arts, the respected critic and promoter of minimalist and conceptual art Ghislain Mollet-Viéville has turned his beliefs and passions into a way of life. His collection of books devoted to art theory and criticism, reduced to the bare minimum and arranged according to artist and era, is housed on shelves behind track-mounted doors. When the doors are closed, the collection disappears.

|1/2| Rare books dealer Michel Bouvier keeps his private collection in a large room at the back of his shop on the rue Visconti in Paris. Order and disorder go hand in hand in this vast space, which serves as office, storeroom and literary salon, and where only bona-fide collectors and book lovers may penetrate. The shelves are made from glass, which lessens the sombre effect of the heavy bindings.

|3| The wooden gallery – a cross between a loggia, garret and theatre balcony – functions as an extra space for Bouvier's treasures.

|1| |2| |3|

|1| |2|

|1/2| It was Christian Sapet's passion for collecting furniture that led him to become an antiques dealer and interior designer. In this warehouse (which looks like a very large and wonderful film set) next door to the Montreuil flea market, Sapet doesn't just construct interiors with his monumental book collection, but recreates scenes from life, from 'the conservatory bookcase of an English novelist' to 'the office of a world-famous Parisian fashion designer'.

|1/2| Metal storage compartments for 'the fabric library of a curator in Lyon', and a pair of modern adjustable bookcases made of metal and bentwood for 'the office of the owner of a primitive art gallery': these two examples are typical of the type of scene Sapet might create to show off his latest acquisitions.

|1| |2|

|1| In the home of a modern art collector, works of art are displayed without pretension, and books are simply stacked up in the recesses formed by a pair of blocked-up doors.

|2| Piled up on a low table and on the floor on either side of the fireplace, books command the space in an otherwise pristine room.

|1| This house in Jouy-en-Josas belonged to Marie-Claude Beaud, the former director of the Musée des Arts Décoratifs in Paris. Each piece of furniture was carefully chosen; the black epoxy metal bookshelves, for instance, were commissioned from Martin Szekely in the 1980s.

|2| Furniture dealer Mara Cremniter, who runs a gallery in Paris specializing in 20th-century examples, built up a personal collection for her loft apartment that includes Alessandro Mendini's Proust armchair, Garouste & Bonetti's Rocher coffee table, an armchair by Jean Prouvé, a Mathieu Mathégot chair, and the Maison du Mexique bookcase, designed by Prouvé and Charlotte Perriand in 1953.

|1| |2|

|1| |2|

|1/2| At the home of a fine-art publisher,
the whole of the main wall in the sitting room
is covered with bookshelves, so that it looks like
a huge painting lit by a few clip-on spotlights. The
two small children's chairs are used as step stools,
while the shelves, made of patinated wood in a
metallic finish, are home to – among other things –
a collection of Multiples by the sculptor Miguel
Berrocal for Artcurial.

|1/2/3| Art historian and conceptual artist Jean-Claude Moineau's apartment is part home, part library. The U-shaped former mechanics workshop contains ten kilometres of shelves that house Moineau's carefully classified archive of the history of modern art. Walking around the apartment is a bit like viewing an installation: the bedroom, kitchen and bathroom have been spared, but the sofas, clothes rails, paintings and other objects jostle for space among the books.

Focus

José Alvarez's LIBRARY OF BABEL

In the grand and imposing private study belonging to the founder of the publishing house Éditions du Regard, books about art sit alongside works of art. While its size, walkways and monumental bookcases scream formality, the elegant refinement is counterbalanced by a modest steamer chair for reading, the simple arrangement of photographs and paintings on the stairwell, and the wide views of the interior garden. It truly is a modern book lover's dream.

Alvarez wanted his working library to be in the great tradition of historical libraries: large, beautiful and galleried. Brought up to date by means of thoroughly contemporary styling, the end result houses all the titles and works of art amassed by Alvarez throughout his career as writer, publisher and keen collector. The *pièce de résistance* is a bronze sculpture of a pile of books by the German artist Anselm Kiefer, situated in the middle of the room.

|1| |2| |3|

How did your book collection come about? I built it up over the years. This particular room is my working library, and it covers all the visual arts. I also have collections of literature and antique books that I keep elsewhere. The collection in here is divided into sections containing artist monographs and exhibition catalogues, on subjects from the classical art of antiquity to the 19th century, photography, fashion, design, architecture, cinema and essays. The 20th-century section contains monographs and catalogues of art movements, including Surrealism, the Bauhaus, Futurism, Actionism and Land Art.

Where do you keep your books? In my study, where I spend two-thirds of my time. I have others in my apartment (my 'emergency book collection'), and still more in other places where I spend time.

How have you arranged them? By subject, and then by alphabetical order. In my other collections, the order is more arbitrary, as I am the only one who consults them.

Are you happy with your book collection? No, because there is always something I want that I do not have, which I imagine is the case with all book collections.

What would be your perfect library? Mine, but ten times bigger.

What is your favourite book collection, either public or private? Jacques Doucet's, which is actually two collections – one of literature and one of books on art and archaeology – although it was put

|1| A true appreciation of the size and beauty of the space requires a climb up to the second, smaller gallery, which overhangs the whole room and is accessible via a staircase.

|2/3| Only two pieces of furniture are allowed in the study: a neoclassical desk, at which Alvarez works, and a Scandinavian-style drop-leaf table, on which are displayed the latest manuscripts, promotional extracts and publications from Éditions du Regard.

|4| |5| |6|

|4| Behind the staircase leading up to the large gallery hangs a collection of famous photographs, while the stairs themselves conceal a set of archive drawers that would not look out of place in an art gallery.

|5| Alvarez keeps a few personal mementoes on the shelves just behind his desk.

|6| The huge, oblong windows – six in all – that open onto an interior garden flood the room with natural light.

together to a large extent by André Suarès and André Breton, whereas I would prefer to do it myself.

Do you keep anything else on your bookshelves apart from books? Yes, works by friends of mine: Helmut Newton, Jean Degottex, Gilles Aillaud, Cy Twombly, Jean-Pierre Raynaud, Anselm Kiefer, Beatrice Caracciolo, Alice Springs, Sarkis, Tadzio Pacquement, Georges Tony Stoll, Erik Dietman, Emmanuel Saulnier, Côme Mosta-Heirt and Jean-Charles Blais, to name but a few.

Where and how do you like to read? Sat at my desk, or on a very specific sofa in my living room. I also read on trains, planes and the Métro, but it's not quite the same.

What do you use to read by? A Jieldé reading lamp.

What do you use to light your shelves? Brass articulated lamps from Galerie des Lampes in the rue de Beaune, in Paris.

What furniture do you have in your study? My desk, a table that I put my books on, and a steamer chair with a footrest.

Does your book collection reflect your personality? I hope so, because I believe a person's books are a reflection of his soul.

Interior designers
AND THEIR BOOKS
COMFORTABLE & DECORATIVE

This library, in the Palais du Marshan in Tangier, was designed by the Belgian architect Robert Gérofi. Although decorated in the Moorish style, with ebony furniture inlaid with mother-of-pearl and a palace lantern, the maps of North Africa and the Strait of Gibraltar on the walls, together with the low bookcases, make the space feel like an old-fashioned English gentleman's club.

The library, that exercise in style for purveyors of the decorative arts, that jewel in the crown of many a prestigious mansion house, château and embassy, is these days a rare commission for the interior architect, with modern clients preferring instead to focus on dressing rooms or kitchens. The 'grand style' of Louis II de Bourbon's library at Château de Chantilly, that of Napoleon at Château de Malmaison, or of Baron de Rothschild at Château de Ferrières is no longer fashionable, and valuable and imposing bookcases have given way to functional storage solutions and flat-packed shelves, which fit with a more casual way of life where books can live anywhere, from the hallway to the bedroom to the kitchen. A few of the nostalgic super-rich can still indulge this dream of the perfect library, and create a baroque reconstruction that dazzles like a cabinet of curiosities, with its precious woods, reading table, rare editions storeroom, perhaps even a mezzanine. Indeed, this type of pastiche worked for Jacques Garcia, who did not hesitate to use faux bois painting and antique busts made of plaster in his own library at Château du Champ de Bataille.

The current trend, however, is to turn the bookcase into a piece of furniture, or an architectural element, like any other, even if it bears the stamp of Fornasetti, Memphis, Charlotte Perriand or Jean Prouvé. It is then either left bare or used to display an array of decorative objects. Another fashionable paradox is the idea that 'arranging' a single book, or a pile of books in the manner of a still-life or vanitas painting, will somehow give the books meaning, and the ability to make an impression with the minimum of architectural decorum.

|1| In his Paris loft, Eric Gizard opts for three simple white shelves on which to display his books and objets d'art. The large dining table is complemented by chairs by Verner Panton for Vitra.

|2| Yves Taralon chose simple, sturdy shelves painted matt grey in place of a sideboard. The souvenirs, ornaments and illustrated books on display bring vibrancy to the dining area.

|1| |2|

|1| Parisian designer Hubert de Vinols has created a reading room in his Auvergne château in the style of a bohemian Louis-Philippe salon. The sombre Directoire-style bookshelves contrast with the eclectic dandyism of the rest of the room.

|2| In the red sitting room belonging to world-famous Parisian hairstylist Alexandre Zouari and designed by Madeleine Castaing, a small mahogany bookcase, lit by a pair of candlestick lamps, evokes a Stendhalian atmosphere.

|1| |2|

|1| The sitting room in interior designer Marie-Françoise Giacolette's 1950s house in Casablanca has the look and feel of a small literary café. Books and art magazines are displayed on shelves against the wall like paintings.

|2| In the Left Bank apartment of German designer Franziska Kessler, a series of bookcases in unfinished wood have been placed at intervals along the main wall of this attic room. The sophisticated simplicity of the design is enhanced by the Japanese-style horizontal arrangement of the books, and the use of plain brown paper folders for filing.

|1| Laure Welfing, a French designer now living in Tangier, keeps her books in this room where the cabinet of curiosities meets scholar's library. Framed by neoclassical columns, the fragrant cedar shelves are filled with antique books and objets d'art. The crystal chandelier in the shape of a sailing ship was designed by the artist Jean-Gabriel Domergue.

|2| This apartment designed by Henri Garelli in Saint-Germain-des-Prés features a large bookcase with a columned façade, flanked by large, bevelled glass panels set into wood panelling. The 1940s furniture provides the perfect complement.

|1| |2| |3|

|1| In his loft in the Bastille district of Paris, Christian Sapet has recreated the look of an old Latin Quarter bookshop, complete with solid wood desk, antique stepladder and Tiffany lamp.

|2| This drawing room, in a London townhouse formerly owned by the Rothschild family, was designed by the British interior designer David Mlinaric. It is a perfect exercise in style, the pale-yellow striped wallpaper providing the backdrop to a fine example of a mahogany Regency bookcase, topped with busts and antique urns in the style of an English garden balustrade.

|3| At Château du Champ de Bataille, Jacques Garcia has installed his book collection in the vaulted gallery of the piano nobile, or principal floor, as was the custom in the 17th century. The room is an homage to an imperial-era library, from the rare books to the positioning of the reading tables, pedestal globe and busts and antique casts.

|1| |2|

|1| On the top floor of a building in the Marais, in Paris, Jean-Louis Riccardi has created a mezzanine to provide extra storage space for books, and filled it with simple shelves in pale grey, giving this masculine sitting room-cum-smoking den the appeal of a bachelor's pad, or the charm and chic of the Paris studio of a rich American.

|2| Set against a background of stripes, Yves Taralon has painted his wooden shelves in ochre and white to look like a window, in a modern interpretation of Empire style.

|1| |2|

|1| At the Cotentin country house of Parisian antiques dealer Sabine de La Morinerie, this charming cabinet, painted in pearl grey, has the romantic feel of Swedish neoclassicism. Some of the panels have been removed so that the books inside can be seen.

|2| In the bright, top-floor apartment of another antiques dealer, Anne Gaillet, white-painted shelves cover the whole of the wall in the study-cum-sitting room.

|1| In this unusual design by Moroccan artist and designer Khalifa El Azzouzi, a white lectern is used to display an art book, giving the effect of a painting hanging in the hallway.

|2| At the London home of Sir Terence Conran, founder of Habitat and The Conran Shop, the library serves as a decompression chamber between the public and private spaces. With its large table covered in green felt, perfectly symmetrical black storage shelves and invisible spotlights set into the ceiling, the room could easily pass for an art bookshop.

|1| |2|

|1| |2|

|1| Interior designer Yves Taralon's holiday home, built into the side of a cliff at Tangier, is accessed via the upper terrace. Here, a traditional Moroccan dresser situated above a small window is used as a storage rack for art and design magazines.

|2| This non-geometric bookcase of metallic painted wood was designed by Eric Ciborowski to store books of different sizes, as well as documents, a sound system, CDs and cassettes. A steel sculpture juts out from one side of the bookcase like a gangway, and serves as a console table and shelf for the small, sculpted desk, also the designer's own work.

HENRI GARELLI'S COSY ENGLISH LIBRARY

Designer Henri Garelli created this English-with-a-French-twist library for his country house, located halfway between Paris and Geneva, where he has his studios. Garelli has designed hundreds of libraries for a raft of prestigious clients, but when it came to housing his own beloved books, he knew exactly what he wanted: a combination of comfort and style. The result is a classic, tastefully decorated room, complete with fireplace, velour sofa, beautiful rugs and soft lighting.

Garelli has given a very 'English cottage' feel to the library in his house in Drôme in Provence, albeit with a dash of French style mixed in. The first-floor room is furnished with panelled bookcases lit by small theatre lamps on the wall, a large, green Victorian-style sofa, complete with a handful of embroidered cushions and a cashmere throw, and a footstool for for both feet and books.

Where do you keep your bookcases? In my country house, set into the wood panelling that covers the walls. The library is more of a winter room, so the fireplace is a central feature. It is on the first floor and overlooks the garden.

How do you arrange your books? The way people arrange their books is often very personal. You can do it alphabetically, or according to subject matter, feelings or preference. I prefer the latter.

Are you happy with your library? Yes, completely happy.

What would be your perfect library? When I create libraries for clients, the design depends on the spirit and theme of the rest of the house. It develops as I take hold of my clients' dreams.

What objects do you keep in your library? Antiques, photographs and books, all placed at random, and from different times in my life. This is where I keep my memories.

Where and how do you like to read? I read all the time and I travel a lot. I usually take a few books with me, and then leave them when I have finished reading them.

What do you use to read by? I have some standard lamps that have black lamp shades with a gold lining. This focuses the light and so makes reading easier, but it also avoids reflections on screens.

What do you use to light your shelves? Small sconces, attached to the pilasters.

What furniture and accessories do you have in your library? Of course, every library needs a table, a sofa, an armchair and lighting, so you can be intimate with your books. In my library, the books, television, DVDs and CDs are all there to provide easy access to cultural pleasures. I also have a few pieces of 18th-century furniture, a 19th-century-style sofa that looks a bit like a large dog basket, some Cogolin rugs, and lots of cushions that I have brought back from my travels. Above the fireplace is a large painting by Bernard Buffet, which picks up the theme of a small sitting room I designed for him and opens up a perspective onto another place.

Does your library reflect your personality? Any book collection is a reflection of the owner's identity, even if what you like most about your books is showing them to your loved ones. My passion for books derives from my childhood, when I used to read in order to escape from a dull existence. Books were my best friends. I was devoted to them, and was then able to transfer that passion to my job as an interior designer. I have had the good fortune over the years to design and build libraries for many book lovers.

|1| The 18th-century armchair is covered in the same fabric as the sofa. Beside it is an occasional table for books and the remote control.

|2| The small theatre lamp with its mushroom pleated shade complements the prints propped up on the shelves.

|3| Standing between two windows that overlook the surrounding countryside, this sombre, mahogany cabinet is used to store Garelli's collection of illustrated books, and to display his rare ornaments. It is kept company by two chairs, both of which are covered in an Indian print.

|4| Two round mirrors by Line Vautrin provide a touch of refinement, while the gold lining of the shades on the reading lamps adds warmth to the light.

|5| The sofa is shaped like a very deep bath, although Garelli humorously refers to it as his 'dog basket'. A throw in camel-coloured cashmere adds to the English charm.

|6| A footstool covered in a 19th-century needlework tapestry serves both as a counterpoint to the large plasma-screen TV behind and as a resting place for books and magazines.

|1|
|2| |3|
|4| |5| |6|

Designers
AND THEIR BOOKS
FUNCTIONAL & ARCHITECTURAL

The point of bookcases, whether they are intended as surfaces or partitions, is to open up space, not obstruct it. This is a problem for designers, who approach their drawing boards with caution, being only too aware of the anti-functional nature of this particular piece of furniture.

As far as these theorists of objects and furniture are concerned, however, one thing is certain, and that is that they take these emblematic pieces of furniture seriously, despite knowing full well that there is no such thing as the perfect bookcase, which has a habit of cluttering and invading space. Since nothing could come close to the bookcase by Charlotte Perriand and Jean Prouvé (the Maison du Mexique bookcase, designed in 1953), postmodern designers refuse to try to compete with this model of modernity, and seek instead to come up with a new vocabulary for shelving systems. Their research is geared towards cutting-edge technology, and their drawings and designs have more to do with architecture, industrial construction, geometry and molecular biology: jacks, sections, scaffolding, ladders, towers, T-squares, cavities and cells. When Dominique Perrault designed the Bibliothèque Nationale, he chose to wear his designer's hat rather than his architect's hat, and came up with the idea of four buildings that resemble colossal books.

Another significant change is that the bookcase no longer has a specific role, but has become multifunctional and open to other uses. Indeed, one can find bookcases in many modern kitchens, where they openly welcome utensils, crockery, household goods, groceries, bottles and spices, along with cookery books.

In the library of his house in the Cévennes region, Pierre Paulin opted for lightweight shelves, attached to simple racks and painted the same shade of blue as his three Groovy chairs for Artifort.

|1| Paulin designed a monumental, pyramid-shaped bookcase to fit the size and shape of his sitting room. Made of white-painted wood, the designer dubbed it 'Milan Cathedral' as a witty homage to the world's design capital. He teamed it with his famous Tongue chairs for Artifort, designed in 1967, and a low, round table, which was the prototype of the one Paulin designed for the private apartments in the Élysée Palace when Georges Pompidou was president of the French Republic. The wall covering, which extends onto the floor, is part of a series entitled *Jardins à la francaise*, and was commissioned by the former French Economic and Social Council. Verner Panton's legendary moulded plastic chair, which stands in front of the bookcase, is similar in shape to the Tongue chairs and also dates from 1967.

|2| This free-standing magazine rack and display stand in white lacquered wood is an original design by Khalifa El Azzouzi.

|1| |2|

|1/2| This bookcase in a loft belonging to Jean Oddes has a metallic theme: grey steel shelves line grey-painted walls, and are fenced in with wire netting, suggestive of a museum storeroom or a high-tech armoire.

|1| Olivier Védrine's study contains prototypes for all his transparent thermoplastic furniture. The neon chair, lace-patterned screen, Blob mirror and sparkling stools all give a futuristic feel to a corner of the room where books on architecture and design coexist happily with a trumeau fireplace, so characteristic of Parisian apartments.

|2| The Bookworm bookshelf, designed by Ron Arad for Kartell, was chosen by Geneviève Lethu for the guest suite of her Île de Ré villa.

|1| |2|

|1| |2|

|1| Reissued by Cassina, this bookcase – designed by Charlotte Perriand for her daughter Pernette – is still in the apartment that was home to Perriand upon her return from Indochina in 1953, and which today is home to Pernette and her husband and partner, Jacques Barsac. Designed to function like a room divider, it resembles a small building with its chromatic vertical partitions and sliding aluminium panels. Pernette has turned it into her own tiny, intimate museum of books on art and architecture.

|2| Italian designer Iosa Ghini, one of the founders of the Bolidismo movement in the 1980s, chose the totemic Carlton, designed for Memphis in 1981 by its founder Ettore Sottsass, to act as both a sculpture and a screen between the entrance hall and the dining room of his house in Bologna.

|1| |2|

|1| In true designer fashion, Christian Ghion decided to prioritize furniture, and filled this room with a collection of iconic chairs by designers such as Charles and Ray Eames and Marc Newson. All that remains of the fireplace are the side niches, into which he has fitted bookshelves.

|2| Elizabeth Garouste designed this cross between a bookcase and a display cabinet, made from unfinished, hollowed-out wood and brought up to date with a coat of bright-blue matt paint, for the office-cum-studio of her house in Ménilmontant, which opens onto the garden veranda.

68 Designers and their books

|1| Looking like part of a chapel or a monastery refectory, this austere bookcase in unfinished metal, with its uprights topped with stars, is an ultra-sophisticated installation by Garouste & Bonetti. It is to be found in a château in the Vendée region, and is typical of the designers' work for furniture firm En Attendant les Barbares.

|2| For some thirty years, artist and designer Christian Astuguevieille has filed his jewelry collections and materials research in the simple, cardboard boxes that line the corridors of his immense apartment like an old Chinese apothecary. The boxes are stacked geometrically on bespoke shelves made of French oak.

|1| |2|

|1| Astuguevieille's library, which forms an antechamber between the sitting room and the master bedroom, is not short on practical details, including these large drawers and small pull-out shelves.

|2| In his modern house on the island of Phuket, next door to the Amanpuri resort, American architect and designer Ed Tootle has opted for a teak interior, with screens and banquettes to structure the space. The reading corner resembles a bar, complete with high storage units and a low, counter-type shelf.

|1| Gaetano Pesce designed this apartment on the avenue Foch in Paris for an aficionado of art and design. One of the mezzanine floors has a huge porthole window and resin ceiling, not to mention this white shelving unit, which, as well as featuring several curved and sloping shelves and interior panels, is also completely unstructured and without an apparent base. All of the furniture is by Carlo Molino.

|2| Stéphanie Marin, the founder of Livingstones (a range of pebble-shaped, modular seating), designed a Mediterranean-style bookcase of whitewashed masonry for her home in Nice.

|3| At the home of Catalan architect Manolo Nuñez, not far from Figueras, shelves filled with books and ancient objects line the walls of a tower that leads up to a roof terrace, creating an esoteric effect worthy of Dalí.

|1| |2| |3|

|1| |2|

|1| Christian Biecher installed his entire personal collection of architecture and design books in the entrance hall of his agency, where it acts as a reference library. The orange chair is Biecher's own design, and the Luxmaster floor lamp is by Jasper Morrison for Flos.

|2| A collection of designer Marco Mencacci's Murano glass vases adds colour to the large, white shelving unit, as do the broad stripes painted on the wall, while at the side, a tubular scaffolding-type structure is used to display interesting objects.

FOCUS

MATALI CRASSET'S ULTRA-FUNCTIONAL SHELVING SOLUTIONS

In this former workshop converted by French designer Matali Crasset into a family loft and design agency, shelving units are used both to define the space and to store ongoing projects, books and files. Crasset, so fond of mixing genres and functions, enjoys the ambiguity of living in her agency and working in her home. In order to avoid partitioning the ground floor, whose large, glazed windows overlook a very green private driveway, a double-sided shelving unit separates work space from family space. On the more private side, built-in shelves provide storage, but also act as a safety guardrail for the staircase that leads up to the bedrooms. Last but not least, the children's bookcase doubles up as a spaceship.

The large shelving unit separates the office from family life via the integration of a sliding door on the left and a lavatory, which opens on both sides, on the right. On the other side, the shelves take on a more intimate role, with a photograph of Crasset's mother on display in the centre.

|1| |2|
|3| |4|

Where are your bookcases? I have several. There is one on the ground floor in the living area, one in the office, one in the basement (which is mostly for files), one in the children's bedroom, and one in our bedroom, plus the large bookcase on the ground floor that separates the work sphere from the private sphere.

How do you arrange your books? They were arranged in alphabetical order, but one day my cleaning lady decided they looked better in descending order of size. Faced with the magnitude of the task of reorganizing everything, we adopted this new classification system, and are only just starting to find our books again now after seven years!

Are you happy with your book collection? The problem I have with books is that they seem to multiply. It's impossible to keep everything, so we end up giving a lot of books away.

What would be your perfect library? One in which a book that I have thought about, dreamt about, is there in front of me. Your relationship with your books is what really matters.

What is your favourite public library? As a student, I used to

|1/2| In the kitchen area, tall industrial shelves for utensils, jars, vases, decorative objects and cookery books demarcate the space and provide some protection for the staircase. As an added bonus, there is no need for a stool to reach the top shelves: you can just climb the stairs.

|3/4| Each compartment of the shelves in the office contains some reference to Crasset's designs.

|5| |6| |7|

|5| All of the desks have been grouped together against the agency's back wall, which has been left blank to create more space and to facilitate interaction.

|6| One of the compartments of the shelving unit has been turned into a small kitchenette, complete with stainless-steel sink, cafetière and bouquet of paper flowers.

|7| The children's bedroom takes up the whole of the first floor of the loft, and has an integrated bathroom pod. The old bunk beds have been turned into a 'lunar module' bookcase.

spend a lot of time in the Bibliothèque Kandinsky at the Centre Pompidou. It opened up new doors in my imagination.

Do you keep anything else on your bookshelves apart from books? In the large bookcase on the ground floor, I keep a photo of my mother, the children's hospital ID bracelets, a few objects by Bruno Munari, including a moiré photo frame and Zizi the monkey, a key, and a pillbox by Nanna Ditzel.

Where and how do you like to read? In my bedroom, at the kitchen table or at my desk.

What do you use to read by? The sun, ideally, coming through the windows in the morning.

What do you use to light your shelves? Natural light during the day, electric light in the evenings.

Is there any piece of furniture or accessory that is essential to you when reading? My glasses!

Do your bookshelves provide a clue to your personality? Yes, certainly, in so far as they contain work by authors and artists that I like. They are a part of me, like another family.

Writers
AND THEIR BOOKS
CHARMING & EXUBERANT

The modern writer's habitat of bedroom or studio is a far cry from Cicero's ideal of a library in a garden, or Montaigne's beloved attic. Writers live surrounded by their own personal libraries, their source of inspiration, until such time as they can afford a separate workplace.

There are two types of writer's office: the overflowing studio of the bohemian creative, filled with unpretentious flat-packed shelves weighed down with books, ornaments, mementoes and heirlooms, with additional books piled anarchically on mantelpieces, tables and floors; and the comfortable library of the middle-class artist, whether it is a formal Victorian study with oak shelving and antique books all lined up neatly, a rustic aristocratic den with beamed roof, or a cosy Proustian-style room with shaded standard lamps.

High at the top of a 16th-century tower overlooking the Périgord countryside, a lover of literature has attempted to recreate a smaller version of Montaigne's literary den, his famous 'attic'.

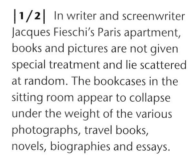

|1/2| In writer and screenwriter Jacques Fieschi's Paris apartment, books and pictures are not given special treatment and lie scattered at random. The bookcases in the sitting room appear to collapse under the weight of the various photographs, travel books, novels, biographies and essays.

|1| |2|

|1| |2|

|1/2| This office also belongs to Fieschi, who has worked with the French film director André Téchiné. The room is lit by an impressive retro light fixture, with shelves piled high with videotapes and DVDs lining the walls.

|1| |2|

|1| In the bohemian apartment of novelist Sibylle Grimbert, the office-cum-sitting room is awash in a tide of novels that the ladder-like shelves can barely contain, and which spill over onto the mantelpiece.

|2| The only concession to comfort is the simple reading chair and small stool in the corner next to the fireplace.

|1| |2| |3|

|1/2| At the former home of Paul Bowles in Tangier, books, mementoes, prints, files and pieces of pottery from Morocco and Mexico are arranged on simple, makeshift shelves. The collection of items is touching in its modesty, and reflects the reclusive life led by the great writer until his death in 1999.

|3| In Bowles's sitting room, books and papers lie stacked up on the low, wooden table, surrounded by traditional Moroccan banquettes. When they are not lying scattered about on the floor, books are stored in the fitted shelving unit, which is typical of the 1950s.

|1| At his home on Paris's Left Bank, novelist and journalist Stéphane Guibourgé's books have completely taken over the dining room. On the family dining table, which he uses as a desk, the traditional bowl of fruit has been replaced by an architect's lamp and computer, while against the wall a large, white bookcase has displaced the customary cupboards and units.

|2| Writer Dominique Souton displays her entire collection of matching novels published by Éditions de l'Olivier, her publisher, in the entrance hall of her apartment. Postcards from friends – bookmarks in waiting – jut out from between the volumes.

|3| This Gallimard author has filled each compartment of the bookcase with two rows of Bibliothèque de la Pléiade books, one above and behind the other, courtesy of wooden shelf inserts.

|1| |2|

|3|

|1| |2|

|1| This writing room, at the home of playwright and 18th-century specialist Bernard Minoret, may look like a novelist's country-house bedroom (and, with its small bed surrounded by bookshelves and other writer's accoutrements, it is certainly reminiscent of Jean-Jacques Rousseau's room at Montmorency), but is actually right in the heart of Paris's bustling Saint-Germain-des-Prés district.

|2| In commentator Sylvie Simon's sitting room, long, white shelves that run the length of the traditional, baguette-moulded cupboards create a harmonious office corner.

JEAN-CLAUDE CARRIÈRE – BOOKS, BOOKS EVERYWHERE

This renowned French screenwriter and author reads and writes in the garden-level rooms of his small, very Parisian mansion house, but makes regular forays upstairs to where his treasured collection of antique books is stored.

When working, Carrière sits at a large, wooden table, facing his wine cellar and with his back to his books, which are housed in old pantry cabinets. There are no books on the ground floor (where the kitchen and the reception rooms are located), but the rooms on the next floor – all except for Carrière's bedroom – are completely full of books, with one room dedicated to classics, another to crime fiction, and yet another to popular literature.

The sitting room-cum-library acts as an antechamber and is furnished with bookcases on every wall, a pedestal table, a red banquette and a rococo chandelier. It opens to the left onto the room that Carrière uses for writing; on the right is the entrance to a Turkish bath. In Carrière's own words, 'You can always tell a good house by its bookshelves, its wine cellar, and its bathrooms.'

How did your book collection come about? I built it up myself from scratch. I did not inherit any of it, or receive any donations. As far as the bookcases are concerned, they are made of wood.

Where do you keep your books? In five rooms in my house. My wife, Nahal Tajadod, keeps her books in the room where she works.

How have you arranged them? Arranging books is always a problem. There is no obvious order. Mine are mainly ordered according to subject, with the more valuable books in a closed armoire to protect them from the sunlight. In any case, a book collection is a living thing; it changes in terms of shape and content every day. One book goes and another arrives; it is like life.

Are you happy with your book collection? I would not say happy, or even proud or satisfied. I am sometimes surprised by it, to the point where I might occasionally have a rummage and find books I had forgotten I owned. And I get on quite well with it. It did tell me off for selling a lot of my books a few years ago, but it has come round now.

What would be your perfect book collection? The perfect book collection would inevitably be incomplete, as well as surprising, disconcerting, and maybe even irritating (if it contained idiotic books). It would contain works from every century, and probably a few undiscovered treasures.

What is your favourite public library? The one I visit most often is the Bibliothèque de l'Arsenal in Paris. I feel very at home there.

Do you keep anything else on your bookshelves? A few pictures, a few mysterious ornaments (presents usually), and good wax for treating and maintaining leather bindings.

Where and how do you like to read? I like reading everywhere, but particularly in planes and trains, perhaps because of the movement. I am less fond of reading in cars, especially when I am driving!

What do you use to read by? I don't have a specific lamp. I read all over the house, and use whichever light happens to be there.

Do you have lights on your bookshelves? No.

Are there any essential pieces of furniture or accessories in the rooms where you keep your books? Just book wax and a stool for the higher shelves.

Does your book collection reflect your personality? Yes, inevitably, as a book collection is a little like a self-portrait. But my books do not know everything about me, nor do I know everything about them.

|1| In the office of this small house in Pigalle, a large table and wooden bookcases with glass-paned doors provide all the luxury of provincial bourgeois comfort right in the heart of Paris. From his desk, Carrière can see through to the wine cellar.

|2| One of the shelves in the antechamber, containing Carrière's complete works and a photograph of himself with the Dalai Lama.

|3| In a corner of the office is an alcove that has been turned into a small reading and relaxation corner, furnished in a contemporary oriental style.

|4| The writer, philologist and book lover keeps his numerous collected works in a succession of small, parquet-floored rooms on the first floor.

|5| A second, old-fashioned desk is kept in one of the upper rooms. This one is darker and lit by two double-suspension Tolomeo lamps by Michele de Lucchi for Artemide.

|1|
|2| |3|
|4| |5|

Fashion designers
AND THEIR BOOKS
STYLISH & GLAMOROUS

A fashion designer's appetite for art books is both irrational and insatiable, and can take in everything from poetry collections to luxurious specialist magazines. While the results of this appetite are usually most evident in the sitting room and bedroom, they will often spill over into the office and hall. Overstuffed bookshelves are par for the course, and are at odds with the perceived frivolity often associated with fashion. Even the fear of appearing obsessive does not prevent designers from ordering their collections fastidiously and storing them out of harm's way.

Couturiers create different effects for a living, so in styling their libraries they may choose at one moment to be a Piranesian baroque antiques dealer, and at another a romantic interior designer, a learned aesthete, a bohemian eccentric or a constructivist artist. Whatever the surroundings, a comfortable reading chair is essential, be it a Charlotte Perriand chaise longue, an armchair by Le Corbusier, a worn-out club chair, or an impeccable Second Empire divan and Chauffeuse chair with matching rug, cushions and footstool. Above all, the aim is to create a space to which overworked designers can retire to enjoy their beloved books.

In his design studio in the Grands Boulevards district of Paris, fabric designer Eliakim stores sketches and paints in a series of white cubes. The overall effect is rather like a dressmaker's shop from a Balzac novel.

|1| |2|

|1| This living room, belonging to Myriam Schaeffer when she was a stylist at Nina Ricci, looks like something out of a doll's house, with its *salon de couture* sofa and shelves that, with their photographs and teddy bears, look straight out of a teenage girl's bedroom.

|2| Parisian couturier Eric Bergère has used designer fabrics on the red walls and pink chairs of his sitting room. A pair of gilt bookcases and a large, ornamental mirror complement the marble fireplace.

|1| A pretty curve of shelves, hung simply and lit by an imitation log-fire heater, adds panache to this minimalist room, which belongs to stylist José Lévy.

|2| This corner of Japanese stylist Koji Tatsuno's former Parisian loft represents salvage in action, from the silver-painted armoire and leather armchair, found in the street and painted gold, to the kitsch prints and improvised bookcase.

|1| |2|

|1| Eric Bergère's old-fashioned former office has retro charm, and shows the young stylist's fascination with the Paris of ages past.

|2| This office belongs to the fashion designer Kenzo, and is on the first floor of the Japanese-style house that he built for himself in the middle of Paris. Walls are lined with light oak panelling, lending the room a classic French feel.

 With its flannel-covered club chair and bookcase half-hidden behind a screen, iconic shoe designer Manolo Blahník's sitting room at his home in Bath goes for a traditional English theme.

|2/3| A copy of an antique sculpture of a foot rests on top of a pile of art books in Blahník's library, while a luxurious display cabinet has been turned into a bookcase. A pair of shoe trees – relics of a bygone age – stand ready to be used as bookends.

|1| |2|

|1| At his holiday home in Avignon in the south of France, floral artist Christian Tortu has chosen wood panelling painted Dior grey for his small, oval sitting room. The bookshelves, fitted into alcoves, are filled with rare books and botanical encyclopedias.

|2| Belgian designer Martin Margiela's taste combines simplicity with caprice. He is fond of painting everything white to create a neutral background, and to divert objects from their intended use. Here, the fireplace has been turned into a bookcase for magazines.

|1| Shoe designer Georgina Goodman came up with the idea for this bookcase-cum-clothes rail in her London flat. On one side she keeps her books; on the other, her clothes and shoes.

|2| Everyone knows that Sonia Rykiel loves both books and the colour black: black carpet, black velour sofa, black walls. The very long, floating shelves in the living room of her apartment on the rue des Saints-Pères in Paris, however, are made of chic light oak.

|1| |2|

|1| |2| |3|

|1/2/3| Thoroughly modern Popy Moreni has gone for an Italian baroque look in her library. There is the faintest hint of a chapel – perhaps dedicated to fashion? – about the room, with its statues of saints displayed beneath cloches. The final impression created, however, is one of a Fellini-style theatre box, taking into account the cinema projector, the red-and-purple velour chairs, and the collection of small polka-dot mats. On the magazine shelf, a group of formal invitations parade, catwalk-style.

| 1 | This fashion journalist has turned her antechamber into her very own boutique and reading boudoir, complete with a charming camouflage-print daybed and modern glass-fronted cabinet, crammed full of novels. The top of the cabinet is home to yet more books, as well as the latest fashion magazines and accessories.

|2| Stylist Yasmine Eslami opts for 1950s chic with this garden chair in sky-blue rattan, pink rug, and a young girl's dream bookcase, full of fashion books and magazines.

|1| |2|

|1| This chic, ethnic library-cum-sitting room belongs to jewelry designers Rafia & Bossa. A side table displaying decorative objects and sculptures is made from the same dark wood as the bookcases.

|2| Delacroix-style Orientalism for the sitting room of these ultra-refined style icons, whose Paris residence is located between the Moulin Rouge, Musée de la Vie Romantique and Musée Gustave Moreau.

LUTZ'S BACKSTAGE LIBRARY

German-born and Paris-based, designer Lutz Huelle – known simply as Lutz – separates his workshop from his fashion books and collection archives by means of simple, white curtains, like those used on a runway. This is where he comes to find peace and solitude once the show is over. Christian Dior and Yves Saint Laurent might have needed a gilt frame for inspiration, but for Lutz, a former assistant to the minimalist Martin Margiela, the backroom-style feel, and simply being surrounded by stock, is inspiring in itself. A small black divan covered with a white wool rug provides a cosy touch, and is somewhere for Lutz to sit down between fittings, or to rest on the busy days and late nights before Fashion Week.

Lutz uses two white curtains, hung like theatre drapes, to cordon off part of his workshop and provide some privacy. A wall of shoe boxes from the last show towers like a rampart above the floor. At the back is Lutz's garment rail, his private 'clothes-o-thèque'.

|1| |2|

What are your bookshelves made of? Wood. They were all made-to-measure by a cabinetmaker here in Paris. They are simple, practical, large, high, deep and very solid.

Where do you keep them? In a relatively small office, which is a bit like a reference library. I try to only keep what I really need, and I like to be able to focus my mind when I am carrying out research.

How do you arrange your books? By genre and subject. The books I tend to consult most often are within easy reach.

Are you happy with your books and the way they are set up? Yes.

What would be your perfect library? One in which you could always find the right book at the right time, and where the piece of information or idea you were looking for was always close to hand.

What is your favourite public library? The one at Central Saint Martins in London, where I studied – I know it by heart.

|1/2| In the centre of the room, lit by a large workshop light, is a small sofa covered with a white wool rug from the 1970s, perfect for reading and relaxing.

|3| |4| |5|

|3/4/5| Everything in Lutz's library has been scrupulously filed and numbered: fabrics in grey office files; show soundtracks in folders with white paper dividers; reference garments hung neatly on the rail in chronological order.

Do you keep anything else on your bookshelves apart from books? Records, cassettes, magazines, photos that have been slipped inside books, and clothes. And then there are boxes containing fabric samples, zips, fabric test prints and old newspapers.

Where and how do you like to read? On the floor, surrounded by lots of books.

What do use to read by? An aluminium desk lamp from the 1970s, a bit like one you might see in a doctor's consulting room.

Do you have lights on your bookshelves? No.

Is there any accessory that is essential to you when reading? Yes, silence.

Do your bookshelves reflect your personality? It is probably the other way round.

Journalists
AND THEIR BOOKS
INTERNATIONAL & UP TO DATE

Inundated with files and reports on a daily basis, time-pressured journalists may never get round to methodically filing the pieces of paper that routinely mount up on top of and beneath their desks. More voracious readers than bibliophiles by necessity, they are constantly in pursuit of the latest story. Their laptops are the only things that manage to stay afloat on the tide of magazines, files, catalogues and books.

Fortunately, journalists are never happier than when rummaging through a pile of work or a jumble of press cuttings, in an attempt to flush out information or secure that elusive scoop. Their only luxuries and indulgences are photographs of chance meetings, travel souvenirs, inspiring pictures and collages pinned to the wall. There is no time for sentimentality or looking back, since all that matters is tomorrow's deadline. Although the Internet may have reduced this appetite somewhat, journalists like nothing better than flicking through news sources, cutting out articles, and compiling and making notes, no matter whether they are on the sofa, in bed, in the bath, or at the dining room table or kitchen counter. As well as being able to enjoy the pleasure of reading, there is always the chance they will unearth a treasure, in the form of a vital clue or piece of evidence that will satiate their curiosity, at least for a while.

Architectural journalist Christiane Germain recreated a copy room in her home and workshop. The second-floor office features a Costes chair, glass table, a Jieldé architect's lamp, and white storage cubes on both walls.

|1| |2| |3|

|1/2/3| Alexandre Cammas, a busy journalist, restaurant critic and founder of the French culinary organization Le Fooding, has – quite logically – his bookshelves in the dining room. Here, magazines he has written for and his own restaurant guides rub shoulders with newspapers, the latest topical books, and a few amusing objects bought at bazaars. In the stairwell, a set of hidden shelves are home to Cammas's collection of novels.

|1| |2|

|1| This office, in a large riad in the medina of Tétouan, Morocco, belongs to political journalist Abdellatif Torres, founder of the Istiqlal Party. The desk and the three bookcases are made of wood and horn marquetry, and are lit by spotlights. Also on display is a photo of Mohammed V, together with a few party banners.

|2| Journalist and art historian Jean-Louis Gaillemin has gone for charm rather than practicality with this bookcase in the kitchen of his small apartment on Paris's rue de l'Université, near the Musée d'Orsay. On the other side of the room, a dishwasher covered in religious knick-knacks sits beneath a giant Art Nouveau poster.

|1| |2| |3|

|1/3| In the tradition of a 19th-century literary salon, interior design journalist Pamela de Monbrison has turned the bespoke bookcase in her sitting room into an album of family chronicles dedicated to 'the art of living', using photographs and other family treasures passed on by her mother and grandmother.

|2| Sitting on the floor next to the very feminine bookcase, a table that has been fashioned from a tree stump is a handy place on which to rest a few books.

|1| |2|

|1| Art critic François Jonquet's office-cum-library is a throwback to the Bohemian style prevalent in Paris's 9th arrondissement in the 19th century, with its simple shelves, Chesterfield sofa in sea-green satin and covered in ethnic throws, camel-saddle stool and Persian rugs. This tasteful reading cocoon, painted in pearl grey, is the perfect setting for a highly cultured man.

|2| Cookery writer Frédérick Grasser, consultant to the chef Alain Ducasse, takes a free-form approach to gourmet design. This professional-looking magazine rack stands in the corner of her office in the house she used to share with pastry chef Pierre Hermé.

|1| Country-house charm in the centre of Paris: in this bedroom belonging to Jean-Louis Gaillemin, books fill the shelves of an old dresser and totter in a precarious pile behind the door. An antique barrister's filing cabinet adds to the provincial feel of the room.

|2| At his home on the place Saint-Germain-des-Prés, journalist and art publisher Gilles Néret proudly displays his anthology of erotic films on his bookshelves, alongside cigar paraphernalia and a collection of exotic souvenirs. The décor is Simenon-style kitsch.

|1| |2|

|1| In spite of the unimpeded view of the Seine and Notre Dame de Paris from this art director's apartment, one's gaze cannot help but be drawn to the bright-blue display cabinet full of stuffed birds, an unusual object that complements the blue wall-mounted shelves, and recalls the nearby Jardin des Plantes.

|2| Made of glass and aluminium, this lightweight compression-pole shelving system fits in perfectly with the stripped-down décor and architecture of this ultra-modern house, formerly occupied by Christiane Germain.

|1| |2| |3|

|1/2| This library, belonging to women's magazine editor Anne Chabrol, has a very Left Bank feel to it, with its drawings, flannel sofa and collection of Gallimard editions. The book-cover rug is a one-off by Tisca.

|3| Daily papers strewn across a red velour Chauffeuse chair, a Napoleon III desk that has been passed down through the family, an L-shaped bookcase freshly painted in slate grey: this small, private room, which belongs to an investigative journalist, has a cosy boudoir feel.

|1/2| The MDF bookcase, painted in matt grey, wooden table and chair, news report photos and black-felt hat perched atop a photograph frame, along with the piles of CDs and interview tapes all work together to give this contemporary journalist's study a very masculine feel.

|1| |2|

Focus
Valérie Lapierre's
FOUR-ROOM LIBRARY

In this apartment belonging to a journalist and lover of crime novels and rare books, no space is left unfilled. The whodunnits all stand to attention behind the grey sofa in the sitting room, the art books adorn the sideboard in the dining room like a fruit bowl, the steamy literature is on standby in the smoking room, and the intellectual books are where the wardrobe should be in the bedroom.

|1| |2|

|1| Lapierre prefers to read while lying in bed. The caricatures of authors on the wall are all her husband's work.

|2| In the sitting room, behind the grey sofa (a new design by Jasper Morrison for B&B Italia), the old Habitat shelves contain Lapierre's noir novels and date from her student days.

|1| |2| |3|

What are your bookcases made of? Savoy pine. We used modular shelves that extend into the furthest recesses of the apartment. Apart from the bookcase in the sitting room, everything has been built by my husband.

Where do you keep them? No room can escape the advance of the bookshelves, except of course the kitchen and the bathrooms. I would never dream of putting books there.

How do you arrange your books? My method could be described as 'subjective functionality', or 'organized subjectivity', depending on your point of view. I may organize them according to publisher, author, genre, theme; I may even take affinities between authors into account, which can create some daring combinations. But all it takes is for a new book to arrive, or for another to be put back in the wrong place, for all my hard work to be ruined. I sometimes think the books move around by themselves!

Are you happy with your book collection? I like the fact that it is a mixture of the serious and the imaginative.

What would be your perfect book collection? One that reflects

|1| This corner of the dining room is 'Hell', where Lapierre keeps her steamy and forbidden books. A red lantern provides the lighting.

|2| Lapierre writes her articles at a desk beside the bed and the window. Her printer is on a small table at the foot of the bed.

|3| A single, black directional wall lamp by Charlotte Perriand lights up Lapierre's collection of noir novels.

|4|
|5| |6|

|4| A photograph of Freud stands among the psychology books at the entrance to the bedroom. Ornaments are kept to a minimum to ensure that the books are accessible.

|5| Even the dining room is not spared this literary critic's appetite for books.

|6| Books waiting to be read are stacked beside the fireplace in the bedroom, next to a figurine from the science-fiction film *Mars Attacks*, brought back from Japan, and a garland of lights from Tsé & Tsé Associées.

a personality that I would like to get to know.

Do you keep anything else on your bookshelves apart from books?
Postcards, a few drawings and some photos, including one of me with Jim Harrison. There is also a sachet of 'Instant Best-Seller' powder, created by the artist Dana Wyse, but I haven't used it yet because I want to be entirely responsible for my own success.

Where do you like to read? I like reading in bed, when I have plenty of time ahead of me. I read intensely, and often end up laughing, crying or dreaming. When the dramatic tension gets too much, I pay a visit to the fridge, stopping off at the coffee machine on the way.

What do you use to read by? An articulated chrome reading light with a dimmer switch, which is attached to the wall above the bed.

Do you light your bookshelves? Yes, using a mixture of shelf lights and small lamps.

Are there any other essential pieces of furniture or accessories?
Yes, a bed, a desk, a chair, and a computer with Internet access. The only other thing I need is a good book.

Do your books reflect your personality? I am my books.

Artists
AND THEIR BOOKS
UNUSUAL & INSPIRING

The book collections of artists are formed in the image of their owners: by definition unclassifiable, almost elusive. More creative than intellectual, they refuse to be tamed by shelves or other bourgeois tabernacles, where dusty tomes languish as if trapped in purgatory. In artists' homes, books are scattered about haphazardly; they live and breathe happily together. Artists may cherish or neglect their books and the places they are stored, depending on how ostentatious they wish to be about their learning, whether they are 'rebellious' or 'structured', and whether they deal in words, images or materials. No matter if they live in a loft, a workshop, a 19th-century apartment or a château in the south of France, the arrangement of their books is bound to be out of the ordinary; the breath of artistic creation tends to sweep away cultural sarcophagi in favour of perpetual disorder and spontaneous accessibility, in the image of permanent creative dissatisfaction.

Such disorder is often more contrived than real, since an artist inevitably maintains his status through reading. The (exceptional) bibliophile artist may choose to shelter a few favourite books in an alcove or more voluptuous presentation box, but the fact is that very few visual artists have designed original bookcases, as if this design issue had more to do with architecture than with sculpture (something that anyone who has gone through arts college will understand). The improvised shelf beneath the staircase, the antique cupboard found in the street, the minimalist storage solution: all of these decorative features tend to stay out of sight in the workshop, whereas a piece of furniture bought in a moment of madness or a piece of Surrealist bric-a-brac has a much better chance of showing up in the home, be it a studio, a country house or a private mansion.

A well-known modern-art dealer keeps his books in the first-floor corridor leading to the bedrooms in his villa at Bari, in Apulia.

|1/2| Tucked away under the eaves in a recess formed by a blocked-up door, these bookshelves neither take up space nor detract from the wallpaper, which is designed to look like a hanging curtain. Such subtlety allows the works by artists such as Mark Brazier-Jones, André Dubreuil, Tom Dixon and Patrick Naggar to take centre stage.

|1| |2|

|1| |2|

|1| This bookcase, at the home of an artist who specializes in trompe-l'oeil, is so perfectly arranged that it looks like a painting in itself.

|2| Artist Annette Messager's yellow bedroom, at her home in Malakoff, almost resembles a domestic interior painting by Bonnard.

|1| In Messager's loft studio, a bookcase resembling scaffolding makes full use of the height of the stairwell. The landing has been turned into a reading room, complete with a bare mattress placed on the floor like a futon, a lamp by Isamu Noguchi, and a garden pedestal table that has been painted red.

|2| Elsewhere in her home, a blue-painted staircase-cum-bookcase is used to store music, firewood and other odds and ends.

|1| Sculptor César Baldaccini's former office, situated just above his workshop in Montparnasse, contained black leather chairs and sofas by Le Corbusier, Jeanneret and Charlotte Perriand, and a spiral staircase by Roger Tallon.

|2| What was, in the 1960s, Baldaccini's bachelor flat, with its porthole-style opening and staircase made out of aeroplane propellers, later became a storage area for paintings and books.

|1| |2|

|1| Roger Vivier, the famous shoe designer, started the fashion for mixing styles of décor in the various houses in which he lived throughout his life. Here, in his Aubeterre-sur-Dronne château in the Périgord region, the huge sitting-room shelves are home to an assortment of archaeological and other objects, including an 'expanded shoe' given to him by César Baldaccini. The paintings on the walls are by Jean-Pierre Pincemin and Eugène Viala, while the chairs are originally from Château de Rambouillet.

|2| Avant-garde British artists Gilbert and George file everything obsessively, including this collection of erotic films and magazines, pictured here in an austere-looking room at their home in London's Spitalfields.

|1| |2|

|1/2| These two examples of an artist's bookcase are quite different, yet both are sophisticated in their own way. The bookcase of painter, sculptor and antiques dealer Daniel Hourdé, who lives next to Notre Dame cathedral, has an air of affectation and mystery, while that of Claudio Segovia, a producer and artistic director for music magazines who lives near the École des Beaux-Arts, also in Paris, is simple and elegant.

|1| Artists and photographers Pierre and Gilles have elevated kitsch to an art form in their Porte des Lilas apartment, which is a permanent work in progress. Pictured is part of a bookcase with a back panel in white laminate.

|2| Filing cabinets full of photographs stacked up like pallets on a building site, teetering towers of magazines leaning against the wall, prints propped up like paintings: it has to be a bohemian photographer's workshop.

|1| |2|

|1| This apartment, which resembles an art gallery, belongs to Berlin-based artist Markus Lüpertz. In order to accentuate the pared-down style of the room and heighten the impact of the works of art on display, the bookcases – home to Lüpertz's collection of art books – have been painted white.

|2| In the Georgian sitting room of British painter and illustrator Lawrence Mynott, a column painted in green and gold draws attention to the bookcase.

|1| This modern triptych at the home of Daniel Hourdé comprises two bookcases in unfinished metal, containing most of the artist's books, and a self-portrait.

|2| Jewelry designer Hubert Karaly is a past master in the art of accumulation. In the bedroom of his home workshop, shelves stuffed with books and all manner of objects help screen the bed.

|1| |2|

Focus

RUBEN ALTERIO'S HAPHAZARD BOOK COLLECTION

This workshop in Pigalle is where Argentinian painter Ruben Alterio comes to paint, play the piano, read, draw, and occasionally doze off. Books land where they fall, whether that happens to be on the piano, an antique pedestal table, a shelf in the box room, a small side table or a sofa. Old encyclopedias are piled up next to dog-eared monographs of famous painters, well-thumbed-through magazines, tango sheet music, paintbrush pots, knick-knacks and ornaments. There is no instruction manual, no distinction drawn between different books, no order, no classification. That is a real artist for you.

In the sitting room of Alterio's Paris workshop, everything is as one might expect, with a workbench, a large and shabby armchair, a pedestal table, and shelves that groan under the weight of works of art, assorted objects and art books.

Where do you keep your bookcase? I don't really have one. My books are all over the place: on the fireplace, on a shelf. It depends where they were looked at last. They move around, changing the landscape of the workshop, getting mixed up with my tools. Sometimes I even leave them lying open.

How do you arrange your books? The encyclopedias are in alphabetical order; the other books are just wherever there is space.

Are you happy with your book collection? Yes.

What would be your perfect book collection? One that was not mine.

What is your favourite public library? The Bibliothèque de l'Arsenal in Paris.

Do you keep anything else on your bookshelves apart from books? Photos, drawings, family mementoes. There is no décor in my workshop, just an accumulation of day-to-day things. There is no space anywhere apart from where I paint, and that is all that matters as far as I am concerned. When I need a shelf, I cut a plank and paint it. In my house, it is different; it is nicer. In my bedroom, there are piles of books on the floor that form columns of different heights against the wall. They grow like trees until I make a shelf for them. Books also accumulate on a large round table in my sitting room. Here, in my workshop, there are mainly art books and dictionaries. In my house, I keep literature in the bedroom and art books and catalogues in the sitting room.

Where and how do you like to read? Anywhere. In a chair, on a sofa, even leaning against the piano.

What do you use to read by? Nothing in particular, because I always read in different places.

Do you light your bookshelves? Not really.

Is there any piece of furniture or accessory that is essential to you in the rooms where you keep your books? Proper coffee, my piano (which is a Steinway), and my clarinet. I come from a family of artists and have been playing since the age of nine. My uncle taught me at the Teatro Colón opera house in Buenos Aires.

Does your library reflect your personality? Yes, definitely.

|1/2/3| Books find their way into every nook and cranny of the workshop. Alterio moves them around from one day to the next, depending on what inspired him at the time.

|4/5| At the back of the workshop is a corridor set up like a photographer's darkroom, which Alterio uses as a storeroom for paintings, frames and archives. A simple bunk-bed ladder serves as a stepladder.

|6| Neat piles of books adorn the top of the grand piano, which is protected by an old cloth and lit by a branch chandelier.

|1| |2| |3|
|4| |5|
|6|

Grand houses
AND THEIR BOOKS
IMPOSING & AUTHORITATIVE

Fossilized book collection, bibliophile's paradise or aristocratic eagle's nest? Like museums, the libraries of grand houses are a historical legacy, a luxurious family inheritance whose precious volumes require handling with kid gloves. They are usually to be found in châteaux or mansion houses, but it is possible to find smaller-scale versions in bourgeois apartments, country houses, seaside villas, even mountain chalets. Immediately identifiable by their old-fashioned appearance, they conform to a rigid design code that excludes all whims and personal touches. The only other objects allowed must be part of a family, historical or cultural tradition: hunting trophies, portraits of ancestors or potentates, precious pieces of china.

Since these libraries symbolize knowledge and power, they aim to project an unsentimental elegance. Their unchanging character demands respect. The pomp and pretentious charm of such installations can seduce unsuspecting aesthetes, who, if they are not privileged enough to come into such an inheritance, can always call upon an interior designer to create one for them.

This majestic library, at Château de Serrant in the Vendée region contains some 12,000 volumes. It is still in use by the current owners, as can be seen from the photographs on the horseshoe-shaped desk in the centre of the room. Complete with magnificent Louis XIII oak panelling, monumental fireplace and family portraits, the library has lost nothing of its historic grandeur.

|1| |2|

|1/2| The famous bookcases at Château de Serrant adorn the vast, double-aspect room like large tapestries. In front of each window is a small reading table with a sloping top. A gallery bookcase, accessible via a set of stairs, completes the ensemble. Extra-tall ladders are on hand to enable readers to reach the higher shelves.

|1| |2|

|1/2| Antiques dealer and interior designer Axel Vervoordt lives in this 16th-century château near Antwerp, which he has restored and redecorated, and occasionally opens to privileged clients for private sales. His sitting room is lined with dark panelling and Cordoba leather, in the tradition of a smoking-room, and is furnished with a cotton-covered English-style sofa. The central portion of the bookcase is used to display Vervoordt's collection of Ming china – another great tradition in stately homes – while the surrounding shelves are filled with rare books and other valuable objects.

|**1**| In the palatial home of the eminent Tazi family in Rabat, Morocco, an entire wing has been dedicated to one family member's book collection. While it might look like it comprises old and dusty tomes, the collection is in fact completely modern.

|**2**| The circular library at the medieval Château de Chacenay in the Jura region of France, restored by Viollet-le-Duc, encircles the private apartments like a castle's moat. The neo-Gothic chairs and lamps, sacristy cabinets and stepladder all combine to give the library its romantic feel.

|1| |2|

|1/2| These two bookcase solutions were both designed by Henri Garelli for two villas in Saint-Tropez. In one, Garelli has used niches and arches to create an idyllic, classical style for a home surrounded by vineyards. In the other, light, studded panelling lends a nautical feel to this home beside the sea.

|1| |2|

|1| Grey-and-gold Empire-style columns enhance the
bookcases in the study of this smart Parisian apartment.

|2| This sitting room in this bourgeois house in Tangier has a
nostalgic feel to it. With its bookcase-lined walls, shepherdess
figurines and portrait by Studio Harcourt of Paris, it is not unlike
the small, somewhat dated drawing room of a luxury hotel.

|1| At Dar Djellouli, an 18th-century Tunisian palace that is now a museum, this ornate reception room, complete with baroque château furniture made of gilt wood and red damask, plaster busts and photographs of dignitaries, was once reserved for prestigious guests. Here, the inverse aesthetic of the 'oriental' sitting room, made popular in Europe by scholars at the end of the 19th century, applies. Interestingly, the low bookcases and small display cabinet containing pieces of silver Ottoman armour are more reminiscent of a bourgeois salon.

|2| This library belonging to the president of the Paris Bar has been decorated in a traditional style by the acclaimed designer Jacques Grange. The imposing conference table, leather chairs and bronze lamps are reminiscent of those in the Bibliothèque Nationale.

|1| |2|

|1/2| The cabinet could be Madame Bovary's cupboard full of novels, and the room could be dramatist Pierre Corneille's writing room, complete with rustic sideboard and bookcase. In fact, they are to be found at the magnificent Manoir de Villers, a 16th-century timber-framed house by the Seine near Rouen, which occasionally welcomes a few lucky guests.

DIDIER GRUMBACH'S CHIC, ARISTOCRATIC BOOKSHELVES

When Didier Grumbach, president of the Fédération Française de la Couture, the governing body of France's fashion industry, commissioned interior designer Sylvain Dubuisson to design bookshelves for his Île-de-France country residence, he was seeking a combination of elegance and austerity. The result is a space where novels and books on fashion history are arranged as precisely as if they were shirts and ties in an elegant gentleman's wardrobe. In addition to being beautiful and practical, however, these bookshelves also fulfil the modest, and perhaps egotistical, desire to keep cultural treasures away from prying eyes, as a child might hide away precious objects in a box in the attic. The greatest pleasure in these shelves, therefore, lies in opening them up to discover what is inside, and then shutting them again to rediscover these treasures later.

Built in the style of an art bookshop by Sylvain Dubuisson, the designer behind the refitting of the legendary Paris bookshop La Hune, Grumbach's attic bookshelves are a superb example of functionality combined with elegance. Made entirely of oak shingles, the shelves are part of the corridor that leads to the bedrooms. They are numbered, so as to make it easier to find and classify books, adding a further touch of sophistication.

|1| |2|

Where did your bookshelves come from? In old houses, the bookshelves are part of the walls; they preserve all kinds of timeless records in a definitive muddle. I wanted to create a family home, so I went to Sylvain Dubuisson, whose work I have always admired. He came just once, in the middle of the summer holidays, to measure the attic. One year later he showed me the plans, which did not need a single modification.

Where do you keep them? In the corridor, transformed by Dubuisson, which is the epicentre of the house. Seven bedrooms lead off it. It is a calm place, ideal for reading and intensive computer use.

How do you arrange your books? My largest bookcase is divided into three sections – fashion, art and architecture – and the headings within these sections are arranged in alphabetical order.

What would be your perfect bookcase? One that was on casters and could be locked up like a house, like the first one by Dubuisson that I saw, several decades ago.

What is your favourite public library? Henri Labrouste's reading room at the Bibliothèque Nationale. It is like a monastery.

Do you keep anything else on your bookshelves apart from books? Yes, photo albums, catalogues, travel souvenirs, some small bronze ornaments, recordings of interviews about fashion …

Where and how do you like to read? I mainly read at weekends or when I am in the country. I like to read while lying down.

|1| This ultra-chic country retreat meets Grumbach's need for tranquility perfectly.

|2| Designer Sylvain Dubuisson is a master of the art of sophisticated simplicity. Here, a simple iron latch is used to close the trunk-like cupboards.

|3| |4| |5|

|3/4/5| Mounted on casters, the
individual bookcases be opened and shut
with the minimum of noise. Each shelving
unit has its own showcase, a stand for
displaying magazines, and a reading stool
made of wood and red velour. Once the
cupboard is shut, nothing can be seen,
making these bookcases both space-saving
and ultra-discreet.

What do you use to light your shelves? Spotlights that have been
skilfully fitted by Dubuisson.
**Are there any pieces of furniture or accessories that are essential
to your bookshelves?** Bookends and ladders.
Does your library reflect your personality? I hope so.

Sylvain Dubuisson, what was the idea behind these bookshelves?
Firstly, the books needed to make their presence felt in the house.
Secondly, the client wanted them to fit into what was essentially a
large corridor on the top floor, lit by roof windows. And thirdly, I had
to bear in mind that the shelves would be mainly for art and fashion
books that would be consulted by visiting friends, both for pleasure
and for study.
How are the shelves structured? Books are fragile things, so I have
protected them in simple cupboards that are a bit like large cabin
trunks. These 'trunks' are arranged in pairs, on either side of the three
windows.
What are the main features of the bookshelves? I chose to display
some books flat on sloping lecterns, as well as in the traditional
vertical manner.
What materials did you use? I used French oak, varnished so as to
make the bookcases difficult to date, or at the very least to make them
appear part of the walls.

Conclusion
THERE'S NO LIFE WITHOUT BOOKS

Go to any modern European hotel, new restaurant, chic fashion boutique or trendy bar, and you will find a bookcases there. Often they are real and filled with the kind of books you would find at home, but sometimes they are virtual, in the form of a trompe l'oeil painting or photographic backdrop. Where does this fascination with books spring from? Is it because they have become part of our heritage tradition, and as such are now considered beautiful objects from the past, like a Voltaire chair or a crystal chandelier? It seems very possible, since this sudden trend for decorative bookcases coincides with the dazzling rise of the Internet, a miraculous virtual library in itself.

A spectacular bookcase runs the full length of the corridor in the tea rooms of the Merci concept store on the boulevard Beaumarchais, in Paris.

|1| |2| |3|
　|4|

|1/2/3/4| Four unusual examples of bookcases: a trompe l'oeil photograph in the basement breakfast room of the Rough Luxe hotel in London; designer shelves in the restaurant of the London's Sanderson Hotel, designed by Philippe Starck; a seating area on the first floor of the Paul Smith store on the rue du Faubourg-Saint-Honoré; and a building-site cabin at 104, the new art centre in Paris.

Overleaf In the small sitting room at the Rough Luxe hotel, the fireplace has been removed and replaced by a sideboard that can be used to store books.

It is also possible to see a bookcase as a cabinet of curiosities, a magical, mysterious lair inhabited by that strange being, the book collector, although nowadays bookcases may store many things, from films and videos to textiles and other treasures. But there is more to it than that. The bookcase, like the book, has become the ultimate decorative item because it symbolizes intimacy within a public space. Wherever you are, you are at home. It represents a new kind of refuge and is a universal symbol, understood by all, regardless of language or culture. No other medium can equal the pleasure that can be gained through collecting, reading or arranging books.

Acknowledgments

Many thanks to all of those who opened the doors of their book collections to us.

Special thanks to:
Catherine Bézard, Fréderic Castaing, Anne Chabrol, Nicolas Delarue, Geneviève Dortignac, Claude Dupuich, Sylvie Flaure, Ghislain Mollet-Vieiville, René Julien Praz, Jean-Emmanuel Richome, Jean-François Soler.

Roland Beaufre would like to give particular thanks to the journalists he worked with on some of the visits:
Alexandra d'Arnoux, Jean Pascal Billaud, Marie-France Boyer, Jérôme Coignard, Jacques Dubois, Jean-Louis Gaillemin, Christine Grange Barry, Esther Henwood, François Jonquet, Marie Kalt, Lisa Lovatt-Smith, Mathieu Orlean, Paquita Paquin, Chelita Salvatori.

Translated from the French *Bibliothèques* by Rebekah Wilson

First published in the United Kingdom in 2010 by
Thames & Hudson Ltd, 181A High Holborn, London WC1V 7QX
www.thamesandhudson.com

First published in 2009 in hardcover in the United States of America by
Thames & Hudson Inc., 500 Fifth Avenue, New York, New York 10110
thamesandhudsonusa.com

First published in paperback in 2012

Original edition © 2010 Hachette Livre – Éditions du Chêne, Paris
This edition © 2010 Thames & Hudson, London

British Library Cataloguing-in-Publication Data
A catalogue record for this book is available from the British Library

Library of Congress Catalog Card Number 2010923362

ISBN 978-0-500-29030-9

Printed and bound in China